A DAY in

Aldeburgh
Snape
Orford

Terry Palmer

HERITAGE
HOUSE

First published: April 1996
ISBN: 1.85215.0432

Printed by: J.B. Offset Printers, Colchester
Published by: Heritage House, Steam Mill Road, Bradfield, Manningtree, CO11 2QT

Acknowledgements:
Clifford Caley, Orford
Michael Catterick, former Mayor of Aldeburgh
Clare Foss, Moot Hall, Aldeburgh
Julie Pipe, Snape Maltings
Mrs Strowger, Thorpeness
Penny Sydenham, Aldeburgh Tourist Office
Philippa Wheeldon, Snape Maltings
Maureen Wiseman, Aldeburgh Tourist Office

● Indicates something worth seeing on your day out.

Heritage House also publishes *A Day Out in Southwold, Walberswick, Dunwich* and *Discover the Suffolk Coast, Discover North Norfolk, Discover the Lower Stour.*

Cover: the Maltings at Snape

CONTENTS

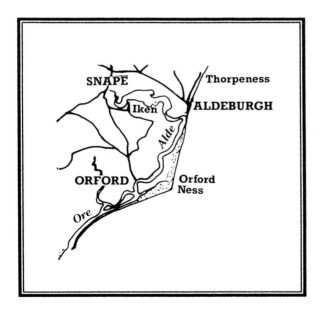

WELCOME!

YOUR DAY OUT around Aldeburgh, Snape and Orford takes you way back into history but also keeps you very much aware of the present day. You have the splendour of Orford Castle - the keep is all that survives, but it was built in the 12th century. You have the charm of Aldeburgh - be like the locals and call it *Oll-brur* - with its medieval Moot Hall and church, and its long connections with the sea. And you have the in-between village of Snape, where a Viking longship was buried 1,400 years ago and where the world-renowned Aldeburgh Festival takes place annually in a theatre converted from a malt-house.

You also have the site of one of the oldest churches in the eastern counties, at remote Iken, and the obvious signs of modern times in the BBC World Service transmitters on Orford Ness, and in the Sizewell A and B nuclear power stations on the northern horizon.

But you need to look at the map for the region's biggest feature, the meandering course of the River Alde, which changes its name to the Ore, and the 15km, 9.3 mile, length of Orford Ness, a shingle spit built totally by wave action and which changes its shape with every new tide.

The lifeboat memorial plaque in Aldeburgh Church

1: ALDEBURGH

TWO BUILDINGS AND THREE NAMES dominate Aldeburgh. The buildings are soon apparent: the church of St Peter and St Paul on your left as you come into town, and the Moot Hall right on the beach. The names are not so obvious: the poet George Crabbe, born here on Christmas Eve 1754, the composer Benjamin Britten, born in Lowestoft in 1913, and women's rights campaigner Elizabeth Garrett Anderson. But that simple statement must not deny the many other people and places that have made Aldeburgh what it is today - a small working town full of charm and character, popular with tourists because it does *not* have a pleasure pier, amusement arcades and kiss-me-quick hats.

The Old Borough. The *ealde burgh*, the original 'old borough,' more frequently translated as 'old fort,' which gave the town its name, was a Roman settlement which vanished into the sea centuries ago. So the river Alde took its name from the town, and really means 'old.'

But here's a mystery. Legend claims the river was originally the Frome, as one of its headwaters rises near Framlingham. But the Ordnance Survey Pathfinder map shows the *Fromus* coming down from Saxmundham. Can this be right? To compound matters, the map marks the stream from Framlingham as the *Ore* - until it meets the Alde, rising way beyond Bruisyard. Can this, too, be right? One thing is certain: in Roman times the river discharged its waters into the North Sea just beyond the town of Aldeburgh.

But the North Sea had other ideas. Ever since the melting of the glaciers, which created the sea, its tides have been nibbling away at the coast of Norfolk and carrying the material southward. Gradually the Alde's mouth was blocked, causing the river to make a sudden turn to the south.

In its early days the town of Orford faced the open sea, but as that great bank of shingle moved slowly past around the time of the Norman Conquest, so the sea gave way to the River Alde. Except that it didn't: the locals called it the River Ore, once more naming it from the town, and over the centuries they watched it turn their little port into a backwater haven. Orford Castle would never have been built if Orford Ness were there in the 12th cent.

The Church. The splendid ●Church of Ss Peter and Paul stands on a slight rise overlooking the town, with a car park beside it (donations welcome). Entry is through a door in the base of the tower, at the west, unusual for Suffolk churches whose door is usually on the south wall. In olden times the north door was kept open during baptisms to let the Devil escape as another child was dedicated to Christ, a custom common throughout East Anglia.

Aldeburgh's original church was Norman, but there is no trace of it today. The present tower was begun in the 14th cent, extended between 1525 and '35 when the chapels were enlarged into the impressive side aisles, giving the interior a square appearance with plenty of space.

Most of the stained glass was 19th cent, and most of that was destroyed by a bomb in 1941, leaving only the large east window - which for long had bullet-holes in it - and three of the other thirteen windows. The **Benjamin Britten window** north-west of the font was dedicated in June 1980 at the start of that year's Aldeburgh Festival and shows Britten's parables written specifically for church performances: *Curlew River* of 1964, *The Burning Fiery Furnace* of 1966, and *The Prodigal Son* of 1968.

Graves and memorials. Britten, who died on 4 December 1976, is buried in the north of the cemetery while George Crabbe whom he immortalised in opera, has a bust in what was the chapel of Ss Clement and Catherine, now the vestry. Peter Piers and Imogen Holst, daughter of Gustav, are buried nearby. Not far away an iron railing encloses Elizabeth Garrett Anderson's grave in the family plot, while her father Newson Garrett has a plaque in the chapel.

Charities. Three local charities are remembered on wall plaques. Mr William Covell bequeathed 13 shillings and 4 pence (66 pence) three times a year, to be spent on bread for the poor; Captain Cheney's Charity left £1 to the vicar and £3 to the poor of the parish; while Captain Hawes's Charity was the most generous, leaving £100 for 'binding out of two apprentices.' No bequest is dated, and all were to be shared 'annually, for ever.'

Lifeboat disaster. Just inside the nave, on the left, is a large ●brass plaque that is, perhaps, the main point of interest for the casual visitor. It recalls, 'in proud and grateful memory' the lifeboat *Aldeburgh* which answered a call for help on 7 December 1899, but was lost at sea with her crew of six, whose ages ranged from 21 to 52. The boat was powered solely by oars and had been on station for 19 years, saving 152 lives.

The church, normally open from 9am to 7pm in summer, stages lunchtime organ recitals during the Aldeburgh Festival, in June.

RNLI and the lifeboats.

The Suffolk Shipwreck Association installed a lifeboat at Dunwich in 1826, but when the Royal National Lifeboat Institution took control in 1851 it opened a station to Aldeburgh, and added number two station in 1905, lasting until 1959. When lifeboats were powered by oar and sail and so couldn't travel far, a string of

Aldeburgh's new lifeboat in its new lifeboat shed

stations developed around Britain's coasts, with more than a dozen in Suffolk. Now that the craft have high-performance motors, the latest in navigation aids, and can stay at sea for days, Lowestoft and Aldeburgh are the sole surviving lifeboat stations in the county.

Look at the present ●lifeboat - and you can, on most days. The *Freddie Cooper*, it's a 12m (38ft) Mersey Class vessel, designed to be launched from a trailer with caterpillar tracks - in other words, from a beach. With a self-righting fibre-reinforced-composite hull and twin 285hp turbo-diesels, the boat has a range of 180 nautical miles at full speed, and still has a crew of only six. For comparison, the rudder of an earlier, oar-driven boat is on display at the front of the new boathouse. The boathouse itself, with guy ropes above the roof like a circus big top, is proving to be a tourist attraction in its own right.

The previous Aldeburgh lifeboat was the *James Cable*, named from the coxwain of the *City of Winchester*, the number one boat from 1902 to 1928, although Charles Mann took over as cox in 1917. *City* was powered by sails and oars and was unable to right herself from a capsize. The people of Winchester bought her for £2,640 and in 43 launches she saved 40 lives.

Between *James Cable* and *City of Winchester* came the *Alfred and Patience Gottwald*, named from the couple who sponsored the 17-ton 12.7m boat whose top speed was 8 knots (9mph,

14.7kph) with a range of 100 miles - but she could carry 70 survivors.

Before that there was the number two boat, *Edward Z. Dresden* which, in May 1918, rescued the pilot of a seaplane which split both floats on touchdown. The lifeboat towed the aircraft into Harwich Harbour; seaplanes were based at nearby Felixstowe in the First World War for spotting German submarines.

James Cable. And what about James Cable? Cox from 1888 to 1917, he had received three Silver Medals, making him legendary among lifeboatmen and a worthy companion to Henry Blogg of Cromer.

MOOT HALL.

Aldeburgh's most prominent building is the ●Moot Hall, put up soon after the town received its charter in 1529. The distinctive Elizabethan-style chimney stack was added during the restoration work in 1855, and there was more in 1986-88. As an indication of the rate of erosion, consider that there were two streets between the hall and the sea; in 450 years not only have they both gone, but the hall itself is living on a century of borrowed time as it is on the beach.

A *moot* in Anglo-Saxon times was a group of people meeting to conduct business or maintain order, and the place where they met came to be called the moot hall.

For generations, the first floor of the Moot Hall served as the council chamber, and more recently as the magistrates' court as well. The hall originally stood on stilts with the cambered ground floor open on all sides as a market place. As the sea came closer the market moved out, and the present flint walls were built.

Aldeburgh lost its borough status in 1974, but the town still has a mayor, who presides in the Moot Hall over council meetings, although they have little more significance than parish council affairs. At least, it perpetuates the image created in the opening scene of Britten's operatic version of Crabbe's poem *The Borough*.

Museum. The remainder of the building, on both floors, is now the ●**Aldeburgh Museum**, with access to the first floor (second floor to US readers) by external or internal steps; it is open at some time almost every day for a small fee. The museum has a fascinating display of artefacts from the town's past, including a whale's shoulder-blade, used as a sign on the now-vanished Three Mariners Inn at Slaughden from 1550. The inn was well-known for its connections with smuggling, and a certain Will Lund was a prominent exponent of the trade. There are Neolithic axe-heads, minor treasures from the Viking ship-burial at Snape, relics from World War Two, a collection of photographs, and the story of the town's fishing industry. Fish and ships are remembered in the Aldeburgh coat of arms which features a stylised three-masted sailing ship; the heraldic device was first recorded in 1561 but may have been in use long before that.

SLAUGHDEN. The hamlet of Slaughden used to stand at the spot where the Alde River makes a sharp turn south, at the start of Orford Ness. In Stuart times, the first half of the 17th cent, it was one of England's leading shipbuilding centres, launching some of the country's biggest vessels into the sheltered waters of the Alde. It was a just reward for the ships that Slaughden had contributed to the fleet that went out to harrass the Spanish Armada in 1588.

Fashions are always changing and Slaughden didn't stay at the peak for long. By 1830 Slaughden shipbuilders weren't building 'ships' at all, but were concentrating on 80-ton fishing smacks for the Iceland and Faroe cod banks. These northern waters were so perilous that the craft had to be supremely sturdy. In 1870 a local fisherman, anxious to test the market for fresh cod instead of the salted stuff brought back from the Arctic, decided to drill holes in the side of his boat's hull so he could bring his catch home alive and swimming. The idea didn't work.

Then in 1900 a severe storm sliced away the foreshore at Slaughden and took with it more of the few remaining houses; somebody captured the collapse of the Three Mariners in a photograph. The storm was the end, not only of Slaughden, but of the boatbuilding industry. Today the hamlet has nothing but modern boathouses holding pleasure craft which sail the sheltered waters of the Ore and Alde and seldom venture into the open sea.

Fish. As a reminder that fishing was the mainstay of Aldeburgh's economy for so many generations, the church register reads a little like a fishmonger's stocktaking list: there were families named Carp, Pike, Sammon, Shrimp, Spratte, Turbette, Wale and Whiting - and, of course, Crabbe. The modern fishing fleet is a small collection of open boats launched from the beach and seldom venturing far from land. Due to years of overfishing in the North Sea, their catches are much smaller and are subject to quotas, but you can still get a good choice of fresh fish at the beach on most mornings.

Overfishing is a modern cause of the collapse of the fishing trade throughout the North Sea, from Aberdeen to Oostende. Trade at Aldeburgh - and Orford - began declining in the 19th cent with the arrival of Dutch fishing boats, and was hastened by the loss of Slaughden, the lengthening of the shingle spit of Orford Ness, the digging of Lowestoft Harbour and the arrival there of steam-powered trawlers, and the coming of the railway.

The Aldeburgh Railway. It cannot be argued that the railway itself hurt the fishing trade. Far from it: when the branch line from Saxmundham to the coast opened on 12 April 1860 it began sending much of the local catch to London, as Lowestoft had been sending its herring to Norwich since 1847. Soon Aldeburgh was freighting up to 70 tons of fish, mostly sprats, to the capital each day. The trouble was - the catch was unsustainable

Originally the railway was going no further than Leiston to serve Garrett's ironworks there, as one of the family was a director of the East Suffolk Railway. During the tracklaying the company got permission to extend the line to Aldeburgh, but traffic to the coast was never as spectacular as it was at Southwold. **Thorpeness Halt** opened on 29 July 1914, six days before the outbreak of World War One, to cater for that growing resort, but it wasn't enough. Even a decade ago the population along the line was only 8,000, nowhere near enough to support a commercial railway.

Just imagine what might have happened if the track from Aldeburgh had not been ripped up. The North Norfolk Railway, now dubbed the Poppy Line, survives as a summer tourist attraction from Sheringham on expensive-to-maintain standard gauge tracks, while the line from Wells to Walsingham has been relaid with 10¼inch gauge track, claimed to be the narrowest passenger-carrying gauge in the world.

But the line to Aldeburgh had already gone. The freight service to the town closed in November 1959, although in 1960 the building of the Sizewell nuclear power station gave the line to Leiston a reprieve from the loss of commercial traffic. In 1965 there were only 16,008 passengers going the full journey from Saxmundham to Aldeburgh, or reverse, so the passenger service on the entire line ceased in September 1966 and no trains at all ran from Leison on to Thorpeness and the Old Fort. Leiston's goods depot closed on 7 May 1984, and the spur line now serves the Sizewell A and B power stations exclusively.

SALT.

Salt has been one of the mainstays of civilization from the earliest times until the arrival of refrigeration. In Roman times certain people were paid in salt, hence the word 'salary,' and in medieval Britain a good worker was 'worth his salt.' In banqueting halls the favoured guests were placed 'above the salt' leaving the lesser mortals below it. When the only ways to preserve meat and fish were by smoking, pickling or salting, Aldeburgh needed its own salt-making industry if its fishing fleet were to prosper. The first pans were formed between the town and Slaughden early in the 14th cent, the rough salt being extracted from sea-water by solar evaporation.

Charter. The town proved itself to be worth its salt in 1529 when Henry VIII granted Aldeburgh its charter. Henry had only recently destroyed Snape's Benedictine Monastery, which dominated the area, so the granting of a charter was, in some respect, merely the filling of a power vacuum.

Yet there was soon to be a surplus of power in Aldeburgh as it became a 'rotten borough,' one which returned two Members to Parliament, until the reforms of 1832. Dunwich and Castle Rising were among other rotten boroughs in East Anglia, with members

Slaughden Redoubt: built to defy Napoleon but helpless against the North Sea

either nominated or appointed, seldom winning their seat in fair elections. Virtually every MP in the country for many generations, sold his services to his constituents, and in cases of conflicting interests he who made the highest bid usually won the day.

Edward VI gave all fishing communities a major economic boost in 1548 when he signed the Royal Assent to an Act of Parliament which prohibited the eating of meat on Fridays and Saturdays, with Wednesdays added in 1563. The Act had limited effect as the farming community sent a petition to Parliament calling for a repeal - but there is still a lingering tradition that claims Friday is the day for eating fish.

Redoubt. The entire south-east coastline needed to be protected against the threat of invasion by Napoleon Bonaparte, which gave rise to a series of round forts, Martello towers, each with few windows and with a single door half way up the wall. The British had seen the original *Torre della Mortella* in Corsica (some reports say Sicily) in 1794 and copied its design at every low-lying stretch of coast from Shoreham-by-Sea to Aldeburgh. Those at each end, and in a few strategic places elsewhere, such as Harwich, were made extra-impregnable and were called redoubts.

The most northerly of these never-used defences is just south of Slaughden, its outer wall already breached by the sea and its main bulk under threat. ●Slaughden Redoubt, built to a clover-leaf plan, contains around a million bricks and is open to view by appointment from its owners, the Landmark Trust.

11

Cinema. Most towns the size of Aldeburgh would have let their cinema die years ago, and now be regretting it. Indeed, in the 1970s the owners of the local picture house decided they could not remain in business any longer and gave a closing date.

But Aldeburgh is not your average small town. The people called for a public meeting where they decided the cinema should not die. They decided to form a cine club, which now has a membership of 700, each of whom pays around £12 a year to subsidise the movie house. ●Aldeburgh Cinema Ltd is now a privately-owned venture which operates on a shoestring but which has not only kept the picture palace open but has renovated much of the building; in 1994 the auditorium was restored at a cost of £30,000, helped by a sponsor-a-seat appeal at £50 a time. Among those who helped pay for the 286 seats are Mstislav Rostropovich, Libby Purves of television fame (she lives at Middleton with her husband Paul Heiney), John Gummer (then Minister of Agriculture, Fisheries and Food) and family, and Warner Brothers.

The cinema opened on this site in 1924 and - apart from essential repair work - has never closed its doors. But it's not just a picture house: there's a gallery which can be hired for parties or special events, a video library, and a small courtyard garden. And, of course, the **tourist information centre.**

Many of the buildings along the High Street and Crabbe Street are worth a second or third glance, but some of particular interest are the ●**White Lion Hotel** north of the Moot Hall; the **Brudenell Hotel** at the south end of town, beside the disused ● **Windmill** ; Stephenson's jeweller's and silversmith's shop at the widest part of High Street, claimed to be the home of Britain's oldest and largest ●**amber dealer;** and the ●**watch-towers** on the foreshore south of the RNLI station. No doubt you'll find others of interest.

Up-towners. Trinity House was created in 1514 to establish lighthouses and buoy the channels of England and Wales (and, later, Gibraltar and the Channel Islands). Before then, Aldeburgh people burned barrels of tar on the church tower as a landmark for returning fishermen. Much later, two watch-towers were built on the edge of the beach to see if any vessel wanted to take on or discharge a pilot. *Two* towers? According to legend the lookouts were really watching for ships about to be driven ashore, when rival groups of men, the Up-towners and the Down-towners, would put out in oared boats and race to be first at the scene - to salvage the cargo rather than to help the drowning crew. One of the towers now houses the **inshore lifeboat.**

ALDEBURGH CHARACTERS

George Crabbe. Aldeburgh's most famous son is, without question, George Crabbe, who was born on 24 December 1754 in a house which the sea has long since claimed. Crabbe's father was the local saltmaster, a man who refined salt on his own account as well as collecting the tax from other refiners. With two of his three sons drowned, Crabbe Snr was not sorry when George showed an interest in a shore-based job. Educated at Stowmarket he started his first apprenticeship in Wickhambrook in 1768, came home and was apprenticed again, this time to an apothecary (a pharmacist) who lived opposite the church. In 1771 he started another career as apprentice to a surgeon in Woodbridge. A few months later he went to London, studying surgery but also dabbling with writing and succeeding with neither; he may have starved had not Edmund Burke, the Irish-born statesman, helped him financially.

In 1775, at the age of 20, the qualified surgeon and apothecary had his first literary work published in Ipswich; it was a long poem called *Inebriety*. Drunk with success, Crabbe hurried back to London to cash in on his fame, but failed to make a mark at all until Burke (now MP for Bristol) introduced him to the right people. In 1780 Crabbe published *The Candidate* and spent a short while in Beaconsfield as Burke's house guest - yet in December 1781 he was back in Aldeburgh. Not as a surgeon, nor even as a poet, but as the newly-ordained local curate!

Within months he was on the move again, having been appointed chaplain at Belvoir Castle, Rutland. In 1783 he moved yet again, first to Frome St Quintin in Dorset, then to Beccles, where he married his childhood sweetheart Sara Elmey of Parham, near Framlingham (Suffolk), and published *The Village*.

The Moot Hall is now on the beach

This was his most important work to date, a true-to-life account of the harsh conditions of the working classes of the time, especially in Aldeburgh. Dr Johnson, an acquaintance of Burke, had read and endorsed the poem, which went some considerable way towards making it a success - financial, as well as literary. But Crabbe moved on. He wrote *The Newspaper* in 1785, the year he moved to the curacy of Stathern, Leics. He stayed here for four years, allowing all his three sons to be baptised in the parish church. He met Dr Edmund Cartwright, the inventor of the power loom who was rector of a parish six miles away.

Crabbe was, for once, in clover. But his patron, the Duke of Rutland, died in 1787, and the widowed duchess contrived to get Crabbe appointed rector of Muston, near Grantham, in 1789.

AWOL rector. This was to be his second-longest appointment in any profession anywhere, covering the 15 years to 1814 - yet he was absent without leave for more than half the time, wandering around Aldeburgh, Lowestoft, and back to Parham in 1792. He wanted to settle here, but as his in-laws didn't like him and two of his three sons died, leaving only John, Crabbe thought another move was expedient. He next surfaced in Great Glemham near Saxmundham, living free in a large house, but he took what remained of the family to Rendham, a few miles north, in 1801, spending four years in a house known locally as Lady Whincups. Crabbe was actually here long enough for somebody, in later years, to put a plaque on the house in honour of its famous tenant.

Recall. At this point his bishop had had enough of a wandering rector and recalled Crabbe to Muston, where he stayed obediently until 1814. But still he could not settle. While his address didn't change, his career did: he started practising medicine and surgery, dabbled in botany - and wrote the epic poem which made him truly famous and endeared him, at last, to the people of Aldeburgh. The work was *The Borough,* published in 1810, which told the story of Peter Grimes, the social outcast:

> Thus by himself compelled to live each day,
> To wait for certain hours the tide's delay;
> At the same times the same dull views to see,
> The bounding marsh-bank and the blighted tree;
> The water only, when the tides were high,
> When low, the mud half-covered and half-dry...

Widower. In 1814 his wife Sara died, having grieved for her two lost sons for several years. Her remains are buried in the chancel. Crabbe? He moved on to Trowbridge, Wilts, as the vicar, and made friends with local poets. Crabbe's surviving son John, now married, came as curate in 1816, and George Crabbe, now 61, decided his footloose days were over, although he was to make shorter visits to Edinburgh, Longleat, Bath, Hastings and Bristol. In

1819 he published his last poem, *Tales of the Hall*, then put them all in his *Collected Works* in 1820.

In his later years he was searching again for romance, proposing marriage to one woman and, on being turned down, writing romantic letters to another. He died in Trowbridge in 1832, aged 77. His memorials? There's a tablet in Trowbridge Church, and in Aldeburgh there's a bust in the church, and a street near the sea-front named from him.

BENJAMIN BRITTEN

Edward Benjamin Britten was born in Lowestoft on 22 November 1913 and was educated at Gresham's School, Holt, and at the Royal College of Music. Music was always in his soul and he had no divisions of loyalty to a choice of careers, the problem which bedevilled Crabbe.

Britten worked with W. H. Auden (who was also educated at Gresham's School) for the GPO film unit from 1935 to '37, the organisation which produced several classics about the operation of the Royal Mail, including *Night Mail*, still shown on television. Britten went to the USA in 1939 and stayed until 1942, working on large-scale instrumental compositions such as his *Violin Concerto.*. Back in the United Kingdom, Britten joined Peter Pears and Eric Crozier in founding the **Aldeburgh Festival** in 1948, when he was 34. He was to see the festival expand and become his life's major work - but he still managed other compositions.

The original performances were held in Aldeburgh church and the jubilee hall but, as the festival's reputation grew, it took in the splendid churches of Orford, Blythburgh and Framlingham. The first performance at **Snape** was in June 1967 in an old malt-house converted for use as a concert hall.

Britten had long ago taken Crabbe's character of Peter Grimes and turned him into a successful opera under that title, which he followed with *Billy Budd* and *Gloriana*, the latter written for Queen Elizabeth II's Coronation in 1953. Less ostentatious works include *Let's Make An Opera* in 1949 and *Noye's Fludde* in 1958. Britten was an accomplished musician and composer who specialised in chamber music, orchestral works, and opera.

Britten - and Peter Pears - also lived in Crabbe Street, at Crag House, from 1947 to '57.

Freeman. He became a Freeman of Lowestoft in 1953 and of Aldeburgh in 1962, and received honourary membership of academies in London, Rome, Hamburg, Belgium, Sweden and the United States. He was made a life peer, Baron Britten of Aldeburgh, in 1976, and died on 4 December that year, aged 64.

Other writers. Suffolk attracts writers and artists, but those with Aldeburgh connections include **Wilkie Collins** (1824-'89) whose major works, now mostly forgotten, were *The Woman in White* and *The Moonstone*. **Edward FitzGerald** knew the town well, although he lived in Woodbridge; his claim to fame was his translation from Farsee (Persian) of the epic poem *The Rubáiyát of Omar Khayyám*. You may have heard these lines from it:

> The Moving Finger writes; and having writ,
> Moves on: nor all thy Piety nor Wit
> Shall lure it back to cancel half a Line,
> Nor all thy Tears wash out a Word of it.

Montague Rhodes James (1862-1936) the short-story writer who specialised in ghost tales, stayed in the town in his later years; **Kathleen Hale,** who made a name for herself with her stories of Orlando the Marmalade Cat, called the town 'Owlbarrow-on-Sea' in her book *A Seaside Holiday.* **Sir Laurens van der Post,** the South African writer and explorer, owned a house in town and used a lookout tower as study; **Edward Morgan ('E.M.') Forster,** author of *The Celestial Omnibus* and *A Passage to India,* regularly visited Britten and Pears. **Ruth Rendell,** the crime writer who lives in Polstead, famous for Maria Marten and the Murder in the Red Barn, has links with Aldeburgh. **Julia Lange,** who used to ask "Are you sitting comfortably? Then we'll begin" on her television programme *Listen With Mother,* lives here in retirement.

Snooks. And don't forget Snooks, the dog perpetuated in statue by the Moot Hall. The statue was the gift of a local family in memory of the real Snooks's owners, Dr Robin and Dr Nora Acheson, who had a general practice in town. Dr Nora wrote a fictional smuggling tale, *Up The Steps,* set in Aldeburgh.

ELIZABETH GARRETT ANDERSON.

Aldeburgh's most famous daughter-by-adoption is undoubtedly Elizabeth Garrett, who was born in London in 1836. Although she spent her childhood in Aldeburgh, she settled in the town only in her later years.

She was a remarkable woman who came from remarkable stock. An ancestor who migrated to North America exactly 200 years earlier, founded Lancaster in Pennsylvania. Her father, Newson Garrett, was the son of the man who started Garrett's ironworks in Leiston. This closed in recent years - the ●Long Shop museum now occupies the old buildings.

Newson went to London to make his fortune. There he met and married Louisa Dunnell, whose family lived in Dunwich. Newson didn't grow rich in the capital, so he came home on inheriting a small endowment from his father. Adding to this some money from the Dunnells, he bought a corn and coal warehouse at Snape, and converted them into the ●**Snape Maltings.** He settled in Aldeburgh, in the house called Uplands, now a hotel of the same name opposite the church.

Elizabeth, born in London, spent her childhood at Uplands. The second child, born 9 June, 1836, she was not content to stay at home. After meeting Elizabeth Blackwell, who had graduated as a doctor of medicine in the USA and had opened a dispensary in New York, Elizabeth Garrett decided to do the same in London.

Victoriana. She never reckoned with Victorian obstinacy - or had it never reckoned with her? She was barred from every medical college in the country purely because of her sex. The science of medicine had come a very long way since George Crabbe had become apprenticed to a surgeon, but despite a queen on the throne, a woman's place was firmly in the home - with very few exceptions.

Elizabeth found one of those exceptions and began nursing in the Middlesex Hospital. In 1865 she became a Licentiate of the Society of Apothecaries, the first woman on the British Medical Register, which allowed her some freedom to practice, and in the following year she opened a dispensary in Upper Berkeley St, London. A cholera outbreak the next year led to her opening another dispensary in Seymour Place.

Sorbonne. But in 1865, Paris University opened its degree courses to women. Elizabeth graduated from here in 1870, the first woman doctor from the Sorbonne. She could now be the first woman doctor to practice in Britain, and within months she became visiting Medical Officer to the East London Hospital for Children - and a member of the London School Board.

James Skelton Anderson. The vice-chairman of the East London Hospital organised her campaign and, after she topped the poll, she and Skelton married. As she had already joined the women's suffragette committee, she didn't become plain Mrs Anderson: she kept her maiden name to become Mrs Elizabeth Garrett Anderson.

P & O. Skelton was in the shipping business and later co-founded the Orient Line. Eventually this was to merge with the Peninsular (with the final 'r') Shipping Company to form the

The Brudenell Hotel

present P & O.

There was a tremendous demand for a hospital for women, to be staffed by women, so in 1872 Elizabeth opened a ten-bed ward over her second dispensary. Two years later it expanded to 26 beds as the New Hospital for Women in Marylebone Road. Elizabeth was now famous in medical circles, was elected to the British Medical Association and, in 1896, was president of its East Anglian branch.

In 1878 London University began admitting women to all its degree courses, and the London School of Medicine for Women was opened. Elizabeth was soon to be its Dean, retiring in 1892. Over the years the school was extended, moved to Euston Road and, in 1902, incorporated into London University.

Postmaster-General. Meanwhile, this remarkable family challenged other fields. Younger sister Millicent married Henry Fawcett who became Postmaster-General in Gladstone's Government. Widowed, Millicent became president of the suffragettes, turning down the job of running Girton College, a woman's college which Elizabeth had helped establish.

Mayor. The Garrett Andersons retired to Aldeburgh in 1902 and by 1907 Skelton was Mayor of the town. He died in office and, although distraught, Elizabeth agreed to serve out his term, and was elected to the office in her own right the next year - becoming the first woman in Britain to hold the title, and that at the age of 72. She died here on 17 December 1917 in the year in which her son, Sir Alan Garrett Anderson, became Controller of the Navy. And during the First World War Dr Louisa Garrett Anderson carried on her mother's tradition by organising the first Army hospital in France to be staffed by women.

WHAT TO DO IN ALDEBURGH

There are numerous sporting facilities in the town and its immediate surrounds. The King's Field recreation ground is near the roundabout on the way into town; **football** and **cricket. Bowls** is available at Park Road, but call 01728.453400 for a reservation. The 18- and 9-hole **golf** courses are on Saxmundham Road. Four **tennis** courts are on Park Road - first come, first served, if you'll forgive the pun. **Sailing** can be arranged at Slaughden, and you can sail **model yachts** on the boating lake by the Moot Hall. This was an emergency water supply and is still used for monthly training by the fire brigade.

The **Aldeburgh Festival** has a range of associated activities throughout the year, in town and at Snape. The Festival fills two weeks in mid-June, and there is now an Aldeburgh Poetry Festival in town in early November. The box office phone is 01728.453543, Mon-Sat, for bookings and information.

Tourist office. In the foyer of the cinema, phone 01728.453637, open daily Easter to October.

2: THORPENESS

THORPENESS IS ONE of the strangest villages in the eastern counties. Like the new towns of Harlow, Stevenage and Haverhill, it never evolved - it was created by design. Unlike those new towns, Thorpeness is a thing of beauty with some highly distinctive features.

Ogilvie family. Glencairn Stuart Ogilvie inherited the Sizewell Estate in 1907, which contained lands in Sizewell, Aldringham, and a fishing village called Thorpe. In 1910 he set about creating a model village, a community conceived on a drawing board. It had happened at Brantham at the county's southern edge, at Somerleyton on the northern fringe - but they were for workers' cottages. Thorpeness would be an exclusive holiday village for the well-heeled.

He engaged labourers to dig, by hand, the 65-acre lake called ●The Meare, with its scattering of islands. As Ogilvie was a friend of J. M. Barrie, the creator of Peter Pan, the lake was known as the home of Peter Pan, and each of its twenty or so islands is named from a character or other feature from the book.

The labourers viewed the operations with some resentment as they were not considered good enough to walk the same roads as the gentry; they had to come and go across the fields.

Ogilvie engaged others to dig a well to the west of the community, safe from contamination by sea-water. The diggers found clear water 28ft (8.5m) down, most of it filtering in from the new lake, and Ogilvie installed a wind-pump to lift it and a metal tank to store it. As he didn't want unsightly artefacts blighting his village, the wind-pump was a ●post-mill from Aldringham, built in 1803 to grind flour, so the unwanted millstones went into the archway of Boat House by The Meare and pumping gear was installed. Ogilvie was lucky in that he had to lift the water only 28ft as the maximum depth at which a simple suction pump can act is 34ft - go deeper than that and the column of water gives off dissolved gases and collapses.

The mill pumped from 1923 to 1940 although the village never had water from the public mains until 1963. Restored in 1976-'77, the mill is now a **visitor centre,** open daily in July and August, and for a small fee you may climb the steps to the fantail.

The House in the Clouds. Ogilvie didn't want an ugly water tank standing high above Thorpeness, either, so on the suggestion of children's writer Mrs Malcolm Mason, he soon disguised it to look like a house. Mrs Mason suggested the name, ●The House in the Clouds, and became its first tenant. Don't be confused: what appears to be the house, painted red, was the tank; what appears to be the covered-in supports of the tank, sheathed in black timber cladding, was the house. The entire structure tops out at 85ft (26m) and is visible for miles.

The Braithwaite sectional-steel tank was pierced in 1943 by a British shell aimed at a flying bomb, without disturbing the occupants below. The corner was sealed off, reducing the capacity from 50,000 to 30,000 gallons. It became redundant in 1977 and was removed, the extra space becoming more living accommodation. Nowadays the five-bed, 3-bath, 2-recep House in the Clouds is privately owned and not open to casual visitors, but is available for letting as a short-term holiday home for around £150 a night or £550 a week. Call 0171.252.0743 for details.

When you go back down the track to the village, turn left and you'll find a tall archway called ● Westgate. The brickwork of the arch concealed another giant water tank.

The Meare is probably the most appealing feature of Thorpeness, as the village has turned its back on the sea. Here you can go sailing or rowing from half an hour to half a day, from Easter to October, and see a vast amount of birdlife in the process. Or sit at the waterside and feed those birds – swans, geese, ducks, coots, moorhens and the occasional gull. The shops are nearby: **Mearecraft,** selling food and drink, the **Gallery Coffee Shop** which also sells souvenirs, and the **Craft Shop.** Pop in and see the Garuda Room, named from the Balinese bird of safety which also gives its name to the Indonesian national airline.

Church. Ogilvie financed the building of St Mary's Church in 1936 and had it dedicated, not consecrated. As a result it's available for services in any denomination and for social functions. Sunday services have always been held only during the

Westgate, Thorpeness, held a vast water tank

summer although around two thirds of Thorpeness's homes are now occupied year-round. Death-duties forced the sale of the properties, which the new owners had to insulate and heat against the cold midwinter blasts off the North Sea.

Glencairn Stuart Ogilvie died in the 1970s, but the family still owns The Meare, the thatched barn, and a few buildings. Call in at **Aldringham**'s Church of St Andrew and see the main feature inside, a plaque to Fergus Mentieth Ogilvie of Barcaldine, Argyllshire, who 'fell asleep' in January 1918. He was the father of the man who created Thorpeness.

Pub. The village has one of the oldest pubs in the county, the ●*Parrot and Punchbowl,* built around 1600 and occupied by the same family from then until 1834. The pub gained 17th-cent notoriety for its involvement with the smuggling of lace, tobacco and spirits, mainly from the Low Countries, although the Excise Officers knew about the trade and frequently tried to stop it. The pub's records claim that the last excise seizure was of 300 tubs of gin.

What to do in Thorpeness. The **golf** course is west of the village, and there is ample scope for **boating** on The Meare.

R.S.P.B. reserve. The land to the south of The Meare has long been reclaimed from marshland, which was the silted-up remains of another mere which in years gone by had been a northern harbour for Aldeburgh's fishermen. It has for some years been the RSPB North Warren reserve, recently extended to cover 506.5 acres (205ha), and it is open at all times with no fee - but there *is* a warden in attendance. Among the many birds seen here are ruffs, gadwall, woodlark, water rail and nightingale. The car park is at the Aldeburgh end.

Snape Maltings.

3: SNAPE and Iken

SNAPE GREW UP on a crossroads beside a **Viking longship** burial site. It was obvious why the Vikings chose the site: they sailed up the river that was later to be called the Alde (Orford Ness was much shorter in those days) to the head of navigation somewhere west of Snape or perhaps near Sternfield (alright – we don't call this the Alde; it's the Fromus, according to the O.S.Pathfinder series of maps – but did the Vikings care?). They would then have hauled their vessel to the top of the highest land around: as most of the countryside was heavily wooded and they had no scientific instruments they couldn't guarantee they had chosen the actual highest spot – but did it matter? The work would have been arduous enough, rolling the longship's keel on logs.

Once the spot had been selected, the corpse would have been laid aboard, and the entire site covered with earth, another difficult task if there was much standing timber around.

So whose grave was this, anyway? Frankly, we do not know. Carbon dating reveals that the burial happened between 635 and 650, and history recalls that it was excavated in 1862. But archaeology in the 19th cent was an amateurish affair and virtually all we know is that the skeleton wore a gold ring and carried a sword and dagger. And his hair was auburn.

St John the Baptist. The village of Snape grew up near the ship burial site, and was mentioned in the Domesday record. It was on the east-west road from the Old Fort to Framlingham, and the north-south road between Saxmundham and Orford, and a crossroads is always a good place to build a church. No trace whatever, remains of the original church, but the present St John the Baptist's, one of ten in the county with this dedication, was built in the late 13th cent.

And was in ruins within two centuries. Despite its crossroads location, Snape failed to grow. Blythburgh, Dunwich and Orford grew (if only to shrink again), but Snape was not on a harbour. In 1785 the parish merged with Friston to the north-east, but by 1864 there were moves to revoke the merger and restore Snape Church, even though the cost turned out to be £300, enough money in those days to build a row of cottages. After the separation the people of Snape decided further restoration was needed, which cost £420 in 1905, enough to build a large house. By 1920 the chancel was re-roofed and the east end rebuilt, and the restoration was complete.

Until modern times the upkeep of the nave, aisles, and tower, was the responsibility of the churchwardens, while the incumbent priest had to maintain the chapel at the east end from his own pocket. That's why you often see a separate door to the chapel, a smaller structure, and different styles of masonry and roofing.

Priory. Snape Priory was founded in 1155, soon after Nicholas Breakspear became the only English pope and Henry II the first of the Plantagenet kings. It was demolished in 1524 by Henry VIII, the second Tudor monarch, as part of his campaign against the Papacy when he was arguing for a divorce from his first queen, Catherine of Aragon. Thus the priory rose with the growth of Catholic fervour, and sank as 'Popery' became unfashionable. The only trace of it is in the name of Priory Farm, to the east of the village.

Snape Maltings. The large malt-houses grew up at the most sensible point: at the highest point of navigation of the Alde, as dictated by the lowest bridging point on the river. And, of course, on the seaward side of that bridge. We have already seen that Newson Garrett of Aldeburgh bought them as coal and corn warehouses, and converted them into malt-houses. He used the small fleet of barges to transport this new product down to London.

Snape Railway. The spur railway to Snape Maltings opened on 1 June 1859, branching off the main East Suffolk Railway at a point just 1.4 miles (2.2km) away. There never was a station at either end, there being only one industrial customer and no passenger traffic, and horses were the sole motive power. The line, running straight across the watermeadows, kept an even gradient and the only major work involved was building a bridge over the river; today it separates the tidal from the fresh waters.

The line carried up to 17,000 quarters (4 quarters = 1 hundredweight (cwt), 20 cwt = 1 ton) or 212 tons of malt to the main line each year, in addition to that which went out by barge and by road. When the line closed on 7 March 1960 it was still using track laid in 1880. The maltings closed soon after.

ALDEBURGH FESTIVAL.

Benjamin Britten first brought the Aldeburgh Festival to Snape in June 1967, staging it in a disused malt-house converted into a concert hall: the acoustics were supreme.

The 1969 season began on 7 June. And on that night, hours after the opening performance, the malt-house roof burned down. For that season, performances were rescheduled in Blythburgh and other churches, and in Aldeburgh's Jubilee Hall.

The original malt-house was rebuilt as a ●concert hall in time for the Queen to open it for the start of the next season, and to keep its character it still has massive exposed beams in the roof, and several ventilation stacks in the ridge.

Snape is now the home of the Aldeburgh Festival every June, attracting visitors from virtually every part of the world. But the **Snape Maltings Riverside Centre** is a busy cultural centre the year round. The Concert Hall has performances almost around the calendar, while the crafts side of the business closes only for Christmas Day and Boxing Day. You have a selection of places to visit: the Gallery for prints and paintings; Countrywear for outdoor clothing; the Granary Tea Shop; the Snape Craft Shop for gifts; Books and Toys; House & Garden; the River Bar; Maltings Music; and Snape Antique & Collectors' Centre. There is a Christmas Shop which opens every September – and there is self-catering accommodation to rent.

The **Plough and Sail** pub, once popular with maltsters, is part of the centre and runs its own restaurant. There are public toilets and plenty of parking space.

Cruises. Several boats berth at the Snape Quay, and it is the starting point for one-hour river cruises in summer. Times are dependent on tides, so phone first on 01728.688303. Perhaps the most nostalgic vessel is the Thames sailing barge *Ethel Ada* which operates a variety of cruises to suit most tastes. There are day trips to the Ore's mouth at Shingle Street, weekends at sea, and cruises for the birdwatcher, artist, or lover of sea shanties. Pre-booking is essential, so call the skipper on.0468.242753 (mobile) or via Snape Maltings on 01728.688303.

IKEN

Iken is one of the strangest parishes in the country. It has a tiny population, confined to a scattering of farms. It has no school, no shop, no pub, no public telephone - yet it has a ●church. And the church has friends for, when the thatched roof of St Botolph's caught fire on 4 July 1968 and gutted the building, 12 members of the parish raised £23,000 over a number of years to restore the tower and the nave roof, and they're now raising double that amount to complete the interior restoration.

Even stranger, perhaps, is that the church is at the end of a narrow lane, with awkward access beside a private house (rumour claims that Princess Margaret was a visitor here years ago), and with restricted parking space a hundred yards from the church door. And very few tourists ever call.

Butwulf. So what is the secret of Iken Church's appeal? Its history must play a major part, for it stands on one of the oldest religious sites in England. Butwulf was a wandering preacher looking for a home. He came to this beautiful site on the south bank of the Alde, with tidal waters stretching over three-quarters of the horizon, from south to east, and in 647, with royal permission, he founded his monastery here.

Saxon Chronicle. The *Saxon Chronicle* recorded the details succinctly in 654: *...in the year King Anna was slain...Botulf began to timber that minster at Ycean-ho.* Ignore the many variations of spelling Botolph and Iken; the village probably takes its name from the Iceni tribe. The scribe added that the evil spirits who peopled the place (the estuarine mud exposed at low tide) were disturbed by his coming, a noxious vapour was exhaled from the ground and the demons gave vent to terrifying groans. They had dwelt there, they said, a long time, and thought to do so forever. They had no other place to go, so why could not Botwulf seek some other spot, since the world was singing his praises? Botwulf replied by making the sign of the cross and setting them to flight.

A charming story, perhaps indicative of early man's fear of the unknown and of strange places. Thirteen centuries ago the countryside would have carried much more timber than now, and the headland could have been unexplored, covered with dense primeval woodland; Eyke, which isn't so far away, takes its name from the Germanic word for 'oak,' and there are some specimens in that area even now, which are at least 1,000 years old. Add to Iken's image the reedbeds on the mudflats, the booming call of bitterns, the will-o'-the-wisp of marsh gas, and the autumnal fogs, and you have the making of Botolph's evil spirits.

Botolph dedicated his church to St Martin, its patrimony changing only after Butwulf's death, and it is known to be one of the first churches in East Anglia. Babingley, near King's Lynn, had a church around 630 and its creator, Felix, became Bishop of Dunwich around 631, hinting at an early church there. Iken's could have been the region's third - but it was destroyed when the Danes slew Edmund in 870. Edmund was a king who became a martyr and then a saint, and gives his name to Bury St Edmunds where, indeed, St Edmund was buried, although 'bury' means 'town, borough.'

Fame. The world was indeed singing Botolph's praises, for his fame spread to Scotland, to Wales, and even to Schleswig in Germany, where the Slesvig Breviary has a prayer for St Botolph's day, 17 June.

He died in 680 and was buried at Iken, his bones being taken between 963 and 975 to Grundisburgh and, shortly before the Norman Conquest, to Bury St Edmunds. The second church was built of stone around the time Butwulf's remains were first moved, and Iken next appears in history in 1297 when Sir William de Esturmy seized it and built the present church.

Pancake. On your way to Orford, note the **Froize Inn** at Chillesford. Froize is an old Suffolk word for 'pancake.'

4: ORFORD and Orford Ness

MODERN ORFORD is one of the sleepiest villages in the country, and that's its charm. Yet it was an important part of the nation's defences in medieval times and has been involved in recent years with radar, nuclear weapons, and long-wave radio broadcasting.

As you park your car in the village centre, between the church, the post office, the **Crown and Castle** and the castle itself, you have already seen most of the place - except the riverside. But there's all that history to explore, starting with the castle.

Power struggle. Henry I (1100-1135) had given the Manor of Framlingham to Roger Bigod in 1101. King Stephen (1135-1154) gave Roger's son Hugh Bigod, the title of Earl of Norfolk in 1140. It was a mistake, as the monarchy was putting too much power into the hands of a mere baron. Henry II (1152-1189) realised the error and seized some of the Bigod estates, including Framlingham, in 1157. But he couldn't keep them. In 1164 he was obliged to hand them all back, whereon Bigod, Earl of Norfolk, began building his own castle at Bungay - he already had castles at Thetford and Walton (near Felixstowe, but the site is now a mile out to sea), and was claiming rights over Norwich Castle.

Henry II was worried. He had only the castles at Colchester and Eye, plus the disputed Norwich. So he ordered a castle to be built at Orford. Why at Orford? Because the town commanded the entrance to one of the most important harbours along the east coast and could threaten sea-borne reinforcements for Framlingham.

●ORFORD CASTLE

In 1165, a year after Bigod began building at Bungay, Henry ordered the construction of Orford. He appointed as viewers - overseers - Bartholomew de Glanville and Robert de Valoines, both of whom were related to Ranulf de Glanville, the founder of Leiston Abbey and Butley Priory. These two viewers were meticulous in their recording of the construction cost, and we are fortunate that their notes haven't been lost down the centuries. The result is that Orford Castle is the oldest in the country for which we know detailed costings.

Between 1165 and 1173 the expense was £1,413 9s 2d (46p), at a time when a labourer earned a penny (0.4p) a day, and the Royal exchequer may have received £10,000 a year - that's the equivalent of the present Government's spending in England and Wales, and the French Government's spending west of a line from Dieppe to Toulouse (Henry II ruled half of France), for a complete year. But in its first twelve months, Orford Castle drained more than £663 from the exchequer, indicating the importance Henry gave to the work. You can see more of these records, plus a plan of the completed castle, inside the keep - all that remains.

The structure was truly immense and formidable, being comparable with Framlingham Castle for size, and far bigger than Bungay Castle. Yet Bungay was formidable in its own way; it had the strongest walls yet to be built in England, 18ft (5.5m) thick at the base and 90ft (27m) tall. Earl and monarch were each building to intimidate the other.

Barons' Uprising. Henry was also improving Orford harbour and church, and managed to finish the castle shortly before the barons of much of England, and some of Brittany and Aquitaine rose in revolt. Henry had the support of Chester, Leicester, Scotland (which he did not rule), Normandy, the Church and the peasantry. The dispute was over Henry's alleged inability to understand his family, but he won the contest and took his revenge upon Bigod, who had to surrender both Framlingham and Bungay.

Bungay's defences were never tested, and Framlingham and Orford saw military action only once. King John (1199-1216) lost Normandy in 1204, was excommunicated in '09, and had Magna Carta annulled by the Pope in 1215 shortly after he signed it. The barons met in Bury St Edmunds that same year and saw a weak king. In 1216, when John died of dysentery, they offered the throne to Louis, son of Philippe of France. While Louis attacked Orford, Hedingham and Colchester, John's successor, the 10-year-old Henry III, attacked Framlingham, which the Bigod family had recovered in 1180.

Louis captured his three castles, one of the rare occasions since 1066 when a foreign invader has made much progress on these shores, but he was defeated at Lincoln in May 1217 and allowed to leave the country. Orford was back in royal hands, having had its one moment of fame. In 1337 Edward III gave the castle to the Earl of Suffolk and it stayed in private ownership until 1930 when it was given to the Orford Town Trust. In the meantime much of the bailey (the walls surrounding the grounds) had collapsed one night in 1841. The Ministry of Works took over the keep, all that remains, in 1962 and now, as English Heritage, opens it to the public every day except Christmas Day, for a fee.

The castle today. You'll find 20 steps up to the door in the keep, and inside, a further 91 to the top, with three intervening floors. From the main floor you can take another staircase down to the basement and two further halls.

Here, at the lowest point, you find the 30ft-deep (10m) well, and the airy lower hall with kitchen and lavatory - all waste went through holes in the masonry and piled up outside. The upper hall had another kitchen and lavatory, with a rainwater tank above. At roof level the rooms in the three turrets are not open to the public, so you'll not see the bakery with England's oldest glazed floor tiles, but from the top of the castle the view across coast and country is splendid. And so is the view the other way around - on clear days the castle can be seen from car ferries far out to sea, and from the headland by Walton-on-the-Naze in Essex.

●ORFORD CHURCH

St Bartholomew's Church, rebuilt in the 14th cent beside the ruins of Henry II's original, has an impressively large nave and aisles, that seem to flow into one enormous hall, more than enough to hold the entire population of 1,000 in 1327 - yet this large building was for a long time considered to be the lady chapel for the smaller church at Sudbourne. The floor is of stone flags, with ten brasses available for rubbing, at a fee.

Several of Britten's works have been performed here over the years, including *Noye's Fludde* in 1958 and *Curlew River* in 1964. The church frequently holds concerts and recitals, in connection with the Aldeburgh Festival.

Smugglers. Maps in the castle hint that Orford was important

Orford Church could hold everybody in the village several times over

into Tudor times, when ships could still moor near the church, and the sea was accessible. There were 16 warehouses, including the present *Crown and Castle* hotel, and the *Jolly Sailor* and *King's Head* pubs, with the romantic possibility that smugglers could have operated here. The *Crown and Castle* is now the only hotel for miles, and has four-poster beds to tempt people to stay the night.

Elizabeth I granted the town its charter in 1579, making it a borough, so Orford had a mayor until 1886 and *two* Members of Parliament until 1852. Now, the mayor and corporation have gone, Henry II's market is in the car park, the church lost the top of its tower in 1830 (it was repaired in the decade from 1962), the Augustinian Friary is in ruins, and both medieval hospitals have vanished.

The Orford Merman. Are you sitting comfortably? Then we'll begin. The story of the Orford Merman must be even more a fairy tale than that of the Growing Stone of Blaxhall. (Didn't I tell you? The stone in Stone Farm's drive is supposed to grow!) Some 12th cent Orford fishermen caught a naked and hairy man in their nets and took him to the castle where he was fed a diet of fish – other reports said he ate anything. But he never spoke, even when hung by the feet. Eventually the locals put him back in the sea, surrounded by nets, but he dived under them and escaped.

I prefer the story of Richard Grey who, in 1793, decided to convince all of East Anglia that witchcraft was a myth. Few people believed him, and in Orford they reacted so violently they decided to show him that, even if witchcraft was not real, the punishment for it was. They tied him to a stake and piled brushwood around it. Grey managed to escape, vowing never to return to this awful town. He settled in Aldeburgh in 1861 where he drowned, aged 80.

Cruises. From the market place, the road runs gently down to the ●harbour, and a large car park. This is the other face of Orford, from where ships have sailed for centuries. And you, too, can take to the water. The *Lady Florence*, a 35-ton cruiser, plies the waters up to Aldeburgh and down to Shingle Street with up to 12 passengers; the tide dictates whether *Lady* heads upstream or down. Call 01394.450897 or mobile on 0831.698298 for the master, John Haresnape.

Britannia II and *Regardless* run hour-long cruises around Havergate Island. The former is a 27ft former jolly boat serving with R.Y. *Britannia* until 1980, and carries 20 passengers. The latter is an open clinker-built launch made in 1992 for crab-fishing. She carries 12 passengers.

Havergate Island. Downstream from Orford is the two-mile-long Havergate Island, where the avocet returned to nest in 1947. The bird is now the emblem of the RSPB, which owns the island. You may visit it by application to the RSPB via the warden at 30 Mundys Lane, Orford. The launch *October Storm* takes guided tours for all- or half-day trips on specified days April-August. The

Orford Castle cost £1,413 9s 2d to build

island is surrounded by a flood bank and is a paradise for birdwatchers.

●ORFORD NESS

The 'island,' as the people of Orford call the ness, is the loneliest place in East Anglia and one of the least visited parts of England. Until recently the entire peninsula was owned by the Ministry of Defence and out of bounds to the public, but the secret establishments have closed, the National Trust has taken over much of the territory, and people are welcome again.

But no more than 96, and then only on Thurs, Fri and Saturday, and only by scheduled ferry crossing from Orford quay. If you'd like to know what it's all about, book through Peter Weir on 01394.450057. There are up to eight crossings per day with a maximum load of 12 passengers, and fare includes the National Trust entry fee, unless you're a member. The Foreign and Commonwealth Office still holds the northern bulge of the ness, and the Nature Conservancy Council holds the southern spur, leaving the National Trust with the tricky bit in the middle.

Airstrip. The story begins in 1915 when an airstrip was built on the marshy land of the island opposite the town of Orford. If you have a good map you'll see a creek marked, running from the River Ore towards the bulging tip of the ness; this is **Stony Creek,** and it separates the marshy land to the west from the shingle on the seaward side.

When military aircraft outgrew this airstrip, the RAF ceased flying from here and began bombing the place instead, with planes based at Martlesham Heath, an airfield which had begun as another experimental station in 1917. One pilot, probably not unique, is known to have flown 16 types of aircraft over the island. Martlesham was to become famous for its achievement in World War Two, and not only because the legless pilot Douglas Bader was stationed there.

Radar. Before that war started, Orford Ness moved into the control of the Ministry of Supply, but it was the Royal Aeronautical Establishment, based at Farnborough, which was doing the experimental work. Sir Robert Alexander Watson-Watt, the pioneer of radio detection and ranging - radar - had begun his experiments here in 1935, but was soon to find the site unsuitable. The Government bought Bawdsey Manor, near Felixstowe, in 1936 for £24,000 and transferred the radar team there in total secrecy in February that year. Bawdsey was to be the home of radar from then on - but that's another story.

Orford Ness stirred little enemy interest during the war, except for an Italian bomber flying from a base somewhere in occupied France around 1941, which was intercepted and brought down, crashing on the ness. Not one plane from the squadron returned to base, forcing the Italians to conclude that they should leave the bombing of Britain to the Luftwaffe.

Atomic bomb. The Atomic Weapons Research Establishment, based at Aldermaston, took over from the RAE in 1959, using laboratories that it had begun building four years earlier. At the time the work done on the island was highly secret, but it can now be revealed that it involved testing the triggering mechanism of atomic and nuclear bombs. It was highly dangerous work, but did not involve the risk of widespread contamination. AWRE, which at the time of writing still occupies much of Foulness Island in Essex, pulled out of Orford Ness in 1971.

Dewline developments. Overlapping with the atomic weapons research was a joint Anglo-American experiment to develop an early warning system known under the code name of Cobra Mist. It was planned to supercede the Fylingdales radar installation in Yorkshire and even the Distant Early Warning Line, the Dewline, in the Canadian tundra. It didn't work, so the venture was called off in June 1973.

BBC. The BBC was the latest arrival, shortly after the Cobra Mist experiment, using the same building. Cobra Mist's aerials were replaced by a series of radio masts, looking on the map like one-third of a pie-chart, almost a mile in diameter. It is the **World Service** transmitter for programmes beamed to eastern Europe.

Lighthouse. Throughout all the coming and going, Orford Ness has managed to retain a lighthouse most of the time. The first one was built in 1603, using wood, and featured a coal fire for a beacon. Not surprisingly, it burned...downwards. Gradually two lights were established but after the present tower was built in 1792 the lower light was scrapped. The lighthouse is not open to visitors.

Numbers of visitors are restricted because most of the ness has developed into a wildlife sanctuary, the birds believing themselves to be safe from human interference. The plan is that they may remain safe. However, the dereliction you see in the AWRE buildings in particular is not all the result of weather damage. Several people have driven down from Aldeburgh in all-terrain vehicles and left their mark.

Danger! At Snape the current flows languidly. At Slaughden it is noticeable in mid-tide, but not strong. By the time you reach Orford the current surges past quite forcefully, too strong for anybody to risk swimming across to the island. At Shingle Street, at the mouth of the river, the current in the midway stage of each tide, is phenomenal. Thousands of tons of water slide past in total silence, yet going as fast as an average person can cycle. Motor vessels heading upriver into an ebbing tide must do so at full throttle and clinging to the shore; even so, they sometimes appear to be motionless. A sailing boat coming downstream with the ebb, by contrast, looks to have the speed of an ocean racer in the Roaring Forties. The message is clear: **do not attempt to swim across the River Ore**. Supposing you tried, and were lucky to make it - what is the point? From the tip of Orford Ness you have a *hell* of a long walk back - via Aldeburgh and Snape, almost tracing the route we have taken on our day out in this charming part of Suffolk.

The River Ore at high tide at Orford